Pebble™ Plus

Dinosaurs and Prehistoric Animals
Iguanodon

by Janet Riehecky

Consulting Editor: Gail Saunders-Smith, PhD

Consultant: Jack Horner, Curator of Paleontology
Museum of the Rockies
Bozeman, Montana

Capstone press

Mankato, Minnesota

Pebble Plus is published by Capstone Press,
151 Good Counsel Drive, P.O. Box 669, Mankato, Minnesota 56002.
www.capstonepress.com

072011
006231CGVMI

Library of Congress Cataloging-in-Publication Data
Riehecky, Janet, 1953–
    Iguanodon / by Janet Riehecky.
    p. cm.—(Pebble plus. Dinosaurs and prehistoric animals)
    Summary: "Simple text and illustrations present the life of iguanodon, what it looked like, and how it
behaved"—Provided by publisher.
    Includes bibliographical references and index.
    ISBN-13: 978-0-7368-5353-8 (hardcover)
    ISBN-10: 0-7368-5353-7 (hardcover)
    ISBN-13: 978-0-7368-6910-2 (softcover pbk.)
    ISBN-10: 0-7368-6910-7 (softcover pbk.)
    1. Iguanodon—Juvenile literature. I. Title. II. Series.
QE862.O65R533 2006
567.914—dc22   2005020797

Editorial Credits
Sarah L. Schuette, editor; Linda Clavel, designer; Wanda Winch, photo researcher

Illustration and Photo Credits
Jon Hughes, illustrator
The Natural History Museum, London, 21

The author dedicates this book to her nephew Eric.

Note to Parents and Teachers

The Dinosaurs and Prehistoric Animals set supports national science standards
related to the evolution of life. This book describes and illustrates iguanodon. The
images support early readers in understanding the text. The repetition of words and
phrases helps early readers learn new words. This book also introduces early readers
to subject-specific vocabulary words, which are defined in the Glossary section. Early
readers may need assistance to read some words and to use the Table of Contents,
Glossary, Read More, Internet Sites, and Index sections of the book.

Table of Contents

iguanodon (i-GUA-no-don)

A Plant Eater

Iguanodon was a dinosaur
that ate plants.
It had sharp thumb spikes
on its hands.

Iguanodon lived
in prehistoric times.
It lived in North America,
Europe, and Africa about
130 million years ago.

How Iguanodon Looked

Iguanodon was

as tall as a sailboat.

It was about 16 feet

(5 meters) tall.

Iguanodon had a thick tail
and two long legs.
It could reach tall plants.

Iguanodon had two arms.
It gathered ferns
and pine needles
with its fingers.

Iguanodon had back teeth.

It was one

of the few dinosaurs

that chewed its food.

What Iguanodon Did

Iguanodons moved in groups
to stay safe from predators.
Many dinosaurs
hunted iguanodons.

Iguanodons used

thumb spikes for defense.

They stuck predators

with the spikes

to scare them away.

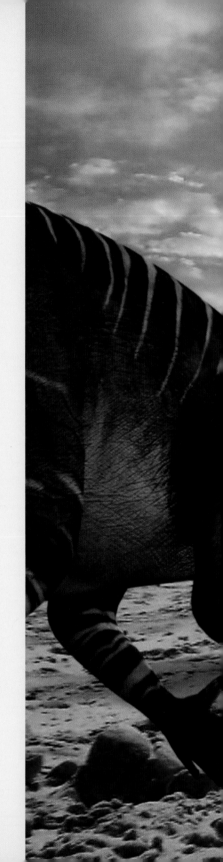

The End of Iguanodon

Iguanodons died about
125 million years ago.
No one knows why
they all died.
You can see iguanodon fossils
in museums.